Our Natural Resources

Jennifer Overend Prior, Ph.D.

Consultant

Caryn Williams, M.S.Ed.
Madison County Schools
Huntsville, AL

Image Credits: p.23 Blend Images/Alamy; p.27 (top) Image Source/Alamy; p.27 (middle) Inspirestock Inc./Alamy; p.28 Jason Moore/Alamy; p.27 (right) Radius Images/Alamy; pp.12–13 Photoshot Holdings Ltd/Alamy; p.20 (background) John W Banagan/Getty Images; pp.6–7, p.24 (top), 24–25, 29 (bottom) iStock; all other images from Shutterstock.

Library of Congress Cataloging-in-Publication Data

Prior, Jennifer Overend, 1963-
  Our natural resources / Jennifer Overend Prior.
    pages cm
  Includes index.
  Audience: Grade K to 3.
  ISBN 978-1-4333-7373-2 (pbk.)
  ISBN 978-1-4807-5159-0 (ebook)
1. Natural resources—Juvenile literature. I. Title.
  HC85.P737 2015
  333.7—dc23
                                    2014010604

Teacher Created Materials

5301 Oceanus Drive
Huntington Beach, CA 92649-1030
http://www.tcmpub.com
ISBN 978-1-4333-7373-2

Table of Contents

What Are Natural Resources?

Natural resources (REE-sawr-suhz) are all around us. Natural resources are things found in nature, such as trees and oil. We use natural resources to make other things. We use oil to make **fuel** for cars and airplanes. A fuel is a source of power. Many houses are made of wood. Wood comes from trees that grow in forests. Some houses are made of bricks. People use sand, clay, and water to make bricks. These are all examples of natural resources.

Wind and sun are natural resources, too. We can use them to make power. We can turn the wind and sun's energy into **electricity**. We use electricity to heat and light our homes.

Oil and wood are natural resources.

Wind turbines and solar panels help us get energy from the wind and the sun.

We need some natural resources to live. Without air, we are not able to breathe. Air is a natural resource because it comes from nature.

People also use natural resources to make things that make their lives easier. Think about some of the things on your desk. There may be paper and pens. Paper is made from trees. Even plastic things, such as pens are made from natural resources. Most plastic things are made from oil. We do not need paper and pens to live, but they do help make our lives easier.

Sometimes, people waste natural resources. This means that they do not use them carefully. If we keep doing this, we will not have these resources in the future.

Capital Resources

Capital resources are the things we use to make something from natural resources. Wood is a natural resource that we use to build houses. But the hammer and nails we use to build the houses are capital resources.

Essential Resources

There are some natural resources that we cannot live without. These are **essential** (uh-SEN-shuhl) resources. We need these things to survive. They include things such as water, land, and trees.

Water is an essential resource.

Water

Water is one of our most important natural resources. We could not live without it. We need water to drink. It is a basic need for all human beings. But we can only drink fresh water that comes from rivers and rainfall. Ocean water is too salty for us to drink.

The plants that give us food also need water. Long ago, farmers learned that they could use rivers to water their crops. They dug trenches in the ground. These are narrow paths in the ground. The trenches brought water from a river or stream to their fields. This is called **irrigation** (ir-i-GEY-shuhn).

Water Mania

We use water every day for many different things. We cook with it. We clean with it. We use it to help our yards and gardens grow. We even use water for fun things, such as swimming and water balloons!

This machine helps farmers water a lot of crops at once.

Land

We need land for **agriculture** (AG-ri-kuhl-cher), or farming. Farmers need plenty of land to grow crops. But they cannot grow crops on all kinds of land. They need land that has healthy soil, or dirt. Land is a natural resource that helps provide us with food.

Farmers grow corn, wheat, and many other crops. These crops help feed people all around the world. Farmers also raise animals such as cows, chickens, and pigs. These animals provide us with milk, eggs, and meat. Farmers need land to raise the animals on.

Think of the things we eat for breakfast. Without chickens and cows, we would not have eggs or milk. Without wheat, we would not have toast or many breakfast cereals. Land gives us the food we need to live.

Trees

Trees are another natural resource that we could not live without. The leaves on trees give us **oxygen** (OK-si-juhn). We need oxygen to breathe. Trees also give us food. Some trees make fruit or nuts that we can eat.

Trees are also used to make lumber. Lumber is made when trees are cut into boards. People use these boards to make houses, schools, and other buildings. Lumber is also used to make furniture, such as tables and chairs. People can also use trees for firewood to keep warm.

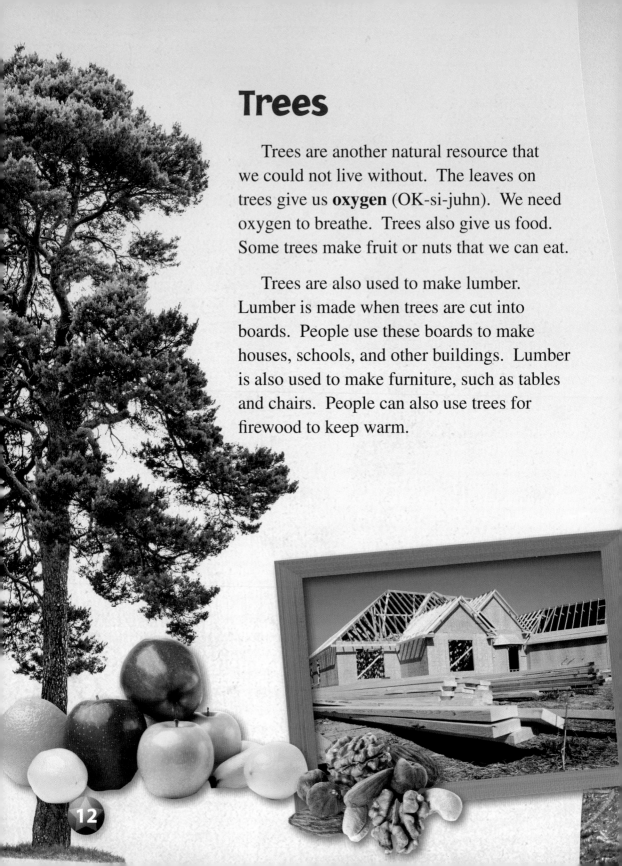

It may seem like there are trees everywhere, but our forests are disappearing fast. This is one reason that people should plant a new tree if they cut one down. This helps keep enough trees on Earth.

Many trees have been cut down in this forest.

Hidden Treasures

On Earth, there are treasures hidden deep in the ground. People dig under the ground to find these important resources.

Oil

Our lives would be very different without oil. It is a natural resource that we use for many things. Oil is a black liquid that comes from underground. Plants and animals that died millions of years ago turned into oil over time. People have to drill deep down to get the oil. Sometimes, they even drill underground in the middle of the ocean!

This oil rig digs under the ground in the ocean to get oil.

No More Oil?

We use a lot of oil! But Earth is running out of oil. We need to learn how to use our oil carefully and find ways to live without using so much oil.

Oil is used to make roads and highways. It is also used to make plastic things, such as water bottles and toys. Oil is a fuel**, too**. Oil is used to make gasoline (gas-uh-LEEN) for cars.

Plastic toys are made with oil.

People use pumps such as this one to fill their cars with gasoline.

Turn Off Engine
No Smoking

92 89 87

Coal

Like oil, coal is a fuel made underground over millions of years. Long ago, dead plants on the ground were covered with dirt, rocks, and water. All of these things pressed down on the dead plants. Millions of years later, the dead plants eventually dried up and turned into coal.

Coal is black and looks like rock. Coal will burn for a long time. In the 1800s, people used coal for many things. It heated water that made steam engines work. Trains used steam engines to move across the tracks. People used coal stoves to heat their food and homes.

Today, coal is mainly used to make electricity. Like steam engine trains, coal heats water to make steam. This steam is used to run the machines that make electricity.

coal

Coal is shoveled into a fire to heat water on a train.

Steam-Powered Trains

In a steam-powered train, people use coal to start a fire. The fire heats water. Hot water gives off steam. Lots of steam builds pressure. This pressure moves the wheels of the train.

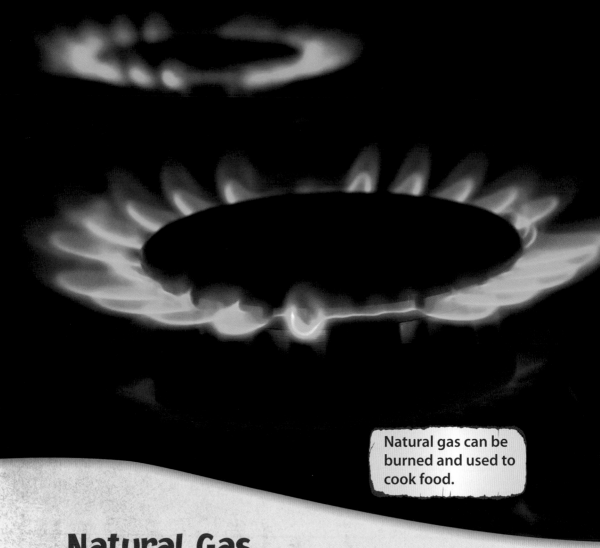

Natural gas can be burned and used to cook food.

Natural Gas

Natural gas is another kind of fuel. Like oil and coal, it is found deep under the ground. It is formed over many years from dead plants and animals that were buried under the sea. Some of these dead plants and animals turned into oil and others turned into gas. The gas is trapped in pockets of rock deep in the earth.

Natural Gas

Natural gas is different than the gasoline that goes into many cars. Gasoline is a liquid that is made from oil. But natural gas is a gas, like air.

Natural gas has many uses. It can be burned as a source of power. Some homes are lit by gas. Stoves and ovens often use gas, too. Clothes washers and dryers can also run on gas. Some homes use gas to run the heater. Gas can be used to keep your home cool, too. It gives power to air conditioners.

People dig for gold at this gold mine.

Gold is used in computer parts.

20

Gold and Silver

People dig in the ground looking for **precious** (PRESH-uhs) metals. Precious means that it is worth a lot of money. We say that a metal is precious when there is very little of it in the world. Gold and silver are precious metals. People have used these metals as money for a very long time. They are also used to make jewelry. Jewelry made of gold and silver can cost a lot of money. This is because these metals are hard to find. That makes them worth more money.

Many computers use these metals, too. This is because gold and silver are good **conductors** (kuhn-DUHK-terz). This means that they move electricity well. Every day, people look for more of these precious metals.

King Tut

King Tutankhamen (toot-ahng-KAH-muhn) is also known as King Tut. He was a pharaoh, or ruler, in ancient (EYN-shuhnt) Egypt. After he died, a mask was placed over his face. That mask was made of 24 pounds of solid gold!

gold bracelet

silver coin

Renewable or Nonrenewable?

Some of our natural resources are **renewable** (ri-NOO-uh-buhl). This means that they can be replaced. Trees are renewable. People can plant new trees to grow. Water is renewable, too. Rain replaces the water that we use.

But some of our natural resources are **nonrenewable**. This means that once they are gone, they are gone forever. If we use too much of these resources, they can become **scarce**. This means that there is very little of that resource left in the world.

Oil, coal, and natural gas are nonrenewable. They will not return until more is made from plants and animals. But this will take millions of years! Precious metals can be used up, too. We need to use these resources carefully or else they will be gone.

Coal and gold are nonrenewable resources.

Trees are renewable resources.

Today, many people are trying to save Earth's natural resources. They do not want them to run out. One way to do this is to use renewable forms of energy. By doing this, we will not waste so many of Earth's resources.

Renewable resources such as water, wind, and the sun can be used to make power. Have you ever seen a **dam**? Water passes through it. Then, the water's energy is turned into electricity. Wind is a source of energy, too. Have you seen a turbine? Wind spins the blades. This motion is turned into electricity. Solar panels turn sunlight into electricity. These are all renewable forms of energy. People can use this energy to heat homes and light rooms.

dam

solar panels on roofs

wind turbines

25

Saving Our Resources

We all need to do our part to **conserve** our natural resources. This means that we need to help save them and use them carefully.

You can help conserve our natural resources. Think about the things in your home. What natural resources does your family use? Most homes use water. You can turn off the water when you are not using it. Most homes use electricity, too. You can turn off the lights when people are not in a room. You can walk to places instead of driving. You can also try growing your own food.

Our planet gives us so many of the resources that allow us to live. We must all make changes to help save our resources.

This girl tells her class to use light bulbs that conserve energy.

Turn It Off!

You can save up to eight gallons of water a day if you turn off the water while you brush your teeth. That is 56 gallons a week!

Recycling is a good way to conserve resources.

Conserve It!

   Think about ways that you can conserve natural resources in your community. Think about what resource you want to conserve. Talk with your friends and family about things you can do to help. Then, write your plan and spread the word!

This boy plants an olive tree.

These kids recycle boxes and bottles.

Using your air conditioner and heater less conserves resources.

Glossary

agriculture—the science of farming

capital resources—things that people use to make goods and provide services

conductors—materials that allow electricity or heat to move through them

conserve—to use carefully

dam—a structure that is built across a river or stream to stop water from flowing

electricity—a form of energy that is carried through wires and is used to operate lights and machines

essential—very important and necessary

fuel—a material such as coal, oil, or gas that is burned to produce heat or power

irrigation—to supply with water by using artificial means

natural resources—things existing in the natural world that a country can use

nonrenewable—cannot be replaced by nature or natural processes

oxygen—an element that is found in the air and is necessary for life

precious—rare and worth a lot of money

renewable—can be replaced by nature or natural processes

scarce—a very small amount or number

Index

Your Turn!

Save Our Resources!

Natural resources are important. We cannot live without them. We must conserve our natural resources. Write your daily schedule. Then, list all the ways you can help conserve natural resources throughout your day. Write them on your schedule.